DATE DUE

COAL

A TRUE BOOK

by
Christin Ditchfield

Children's Press®
A Division of Scholastic Inc.

New York Toronto London Auckland Sydney
Mexico City New Delhi Hong Kong
Danbury, Connecticut

A miner examines
a lump of coal.

Content Consultant
Jan Jenner, Ph.D

Reading Consultant
Linda Cornwell
National Literacy Specialist

Library of Congress Cataloging-in-Publication Data

Ditchfield, Christin.
 Coal / by Christin Ditchfield
  p. cm. — (A true book)
 Includes bibliographical references and index.
 ISBN 0-516-22342-9 (lib. bdg.)   0-516-29366-4 (pbk.)
 1. Coal—Juvenile literature. [1. Petroleum.] I. Title. II. Series.

TN801 .D57 2002
553.2'4—dc21   2001023106

Contents

A piece of coal
from Canada

What Is Coal?

When you first see it, a lump of coal may look like an ordinary rock. However, coal is one of our most valuable natural resources. A natural resource is a substance found in nature that has many important uses. This black or brown rock produces heat and energy when it is burned.

Coal began as plants and trees in swamplands.

Coal is formed by heat and pressure over thousands and thousands of years. Coal is often called a **fossil fuel**, because it begins as a mixture of **decayed** plants and trees. Many years ago, these plants grew in thick, swampy land. When the plants died, they began to rot. As floods, earthquakes, and land-slides changed the surface of the land, these plants were covered by layers of mud and sand. The heat and weight of these layers squeezed all the water out of the rotting plants. As the plant material dried out, it became thicker and harder.

Slowly the rotting plants turned into peat. Pieces of peat look just like rotted wood. They are dark brown and chunky. Later, layers of peat were buried by more layers of rocks, shells, and sand. Over time, the peat hardened into coal.

Peat can be found in swamps and other places.

Where Is Coal Found?

Coal is the most plentiful fossil fuel. It can be found on every continent around the world. More than three-fourths of the Earth's coal deposits are located in Russia, the United States, and China. **Geologists** have also found large amounts of coal in Canada and Western Europe.

A coal seam in a cliff in Alaska

Geologists are scientists who study rocks and minerals. Geologists tell us that coal is buried deep below Earth's surface in layers called seams.

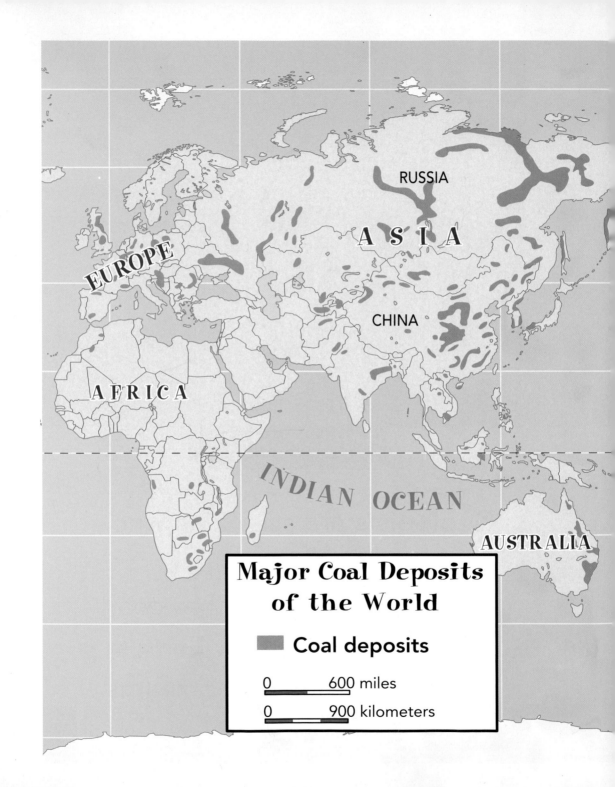

RUSSIA

A S I A

EUROPE

CHINA

AFRICA

INDIAN OCEAN

AUSTRALIA

Major Coal Deposits of the World

■ Coal deposits

0   600 miles

0   900 kilometers

NORTH CANADA
AMERICA

UNITED STATES
OF AMERICA

PACIFIC

ATLANTIC

Equator

OCEAN

SOUTH
AMERICA

OCEAN

N
W E
S

Coal seams are pressed between layers of other types of rocks and soil. It takes several feet of crushed plant material to form a coal seam that is only 12 inches (30 centimeters) thick. Coal seams come in many different sizes. Some layers are very thin. Others are very thick. China has the largest coal seam ever found. This seam measures more than 400 feet (122 meters) thick.

That's bigger than a football field!

In some places, there are layers and layers of coal stacked on top of each other. Layers may be broken or rearranged by earthquakes and other movements in the ground. Different types of coal come from different seams. The more the seam has been pressed, the harder its coal will be.

Close to the Earth's surface, geologists find lignite. Lignite

Look at the differences between a piece of lignite coal (right) and a piece of cannel coal (below).

is a soft, dark brown coal that crumbles easily. It feels a little like wood. At deeper levels, the coal seams are made of cannel. This thick, oily kind of coal is harder than lignite. But it is still weak and breakable.

Bituminous coal is the most common type of coal. It comes from seams that are even deeper below the Earth's surface. This coal may be dark gray or black. It burns with a yellow, smoky flame. For centuries, people

A close-up photograph of bituminous coal

have used bituminous coal as **fuel** to heat their homes and provide power for their factories.

Anthracite is the hardest, rarest, and most expensive coal. It comes from the deepest underground layers. This black coal looks shiny. It burns slowly, with almost no smoke. The largest anthracite coal deposits in the world are found in Pennsylvania.

Anthracite is sometimes called peacock coal.

Fun Facts About Coal

Queen Victoria

For thousands of years, people have worn jewelry made of coal! This type of coal is called jet. It looks like shiny black glass, but jet is soft and easy to carve. Jewelers have shaped jet into buttons, pins, bracelets, and necklaces. Queen Victoria ruled Great Britain from 1837 to 1901. This famous queen wore a lot of jet jewelry. It became very popular in England during the 1860s.

How Is Coal Processed?

Most types of coal lie buried under Earth's surface. For hundreds of years, people have used picks and shovels to dig up coal. Miners began by digging tunnels deep into the ground to reach the coal seams below. They climbed down into the tunnels and

A worker shovels coal.

cut the coal with pick-axes. Then they loaded the coal into wagons or carts and pushed it up to the surface. Sometimes the tunnels—called shafts— were small and narrow. In the past, little children were often sent down into the shafts to push the carts. This kind of coal mining was hard and dangerous work.

In time, scientists invented machines to help the miners. Now, there are all kinds of

A special drill
helps miners to
dig out coal.

special drills and cutters. Computers operate most of the equipment. Also, most mines have offices, work-shops, and rest rooms as well as places for workers to rest and eat. Today, all the miners are adults who are specially trained to do their jobs. They wear protective clothing and hard helmets with lights attached. Goggles keep the coal dust from getting into their eyes.

Miners now use elevators to go up and down the shaft. Coal cars take them to whichever part of the mine they are working on each day. When the coal has been cut, it is placed on **conveyor belts**. These conveyor belts bring the coal to the coal trains and shuttle cars. Then the shuttle cars carry the coal to the surface of the mine. At the surface, workers load the coal onto

Miners wait in an elevator to go down into the mine.

A truck takes away a load of coal.

big trucks. The trucks take the coal to factories where it will be cleaned and prepared for use.

Sometimes, miners do not have to dig very deep to reach a coal seam. If the coal is near the surface, it can be uncovered by surface, or strip, mining. Bulldozers remove the top layer of rocks and soil. Miners dig up the coal and cut it out of the ground. Then the bulldozers cover up the ground by replacing the rocks and soil.

This machine called a double-decker drill is used in strip mining.

On the Job

Working in a mine is a tough job.

Coal mining can be a dangerous job! Mines are dark and dirty. Sometimes underground digging releases poisonous gas that can make workers sick. Breathing coal dust all day can cause lung problems. Many miners have been trapped and killed when the tunnels they worked in collapsed on them.

Fortunately, mining companies have found ways to make the job safer. Much of the hardest work is now done by machines. Metal supports are built into the mine shafts to hold the walls in place and pillars keep the ceilings from collapsing. Workers wear special clothing that protects them from some of the dangers. They have learned ways to avoid accidents. Mining is still a tough job, but it is a lot safer than it used to be!

What Is Coal Used For?

Coal has always been an important source of fuel. People burn coal in stoves and furnaces to heat their homes during winter. Power plants burn coal to create energy. There, the heat and steam from the burning coal drives machines called turbines and

Coal is a source of fuel. This man shovels coal into the engine to power the train.

generators. Turbines and generators are engines that are powered by water, steam, or gas. They create electricity. For years, trains and steamboats were powered by coal.

Coal is not just a fuel, though. It has many other uses. When coal is heated, it forms a substance called coke. Coke is used to make steel and iron. Some medicines, soaps, and **detergents** are made from coal. Coal can be found in ink, glue, and shoe polish. It is used in weed killers and fertilizers. Even some perfumes and nail polishes contain coal. Most plastic and nylon items come from coal products. These

Coal can be found in many things, including glue and nail polish.

items range from buckets and bottles to dolls and building blocks as well as kites, tents, and sports clothing.

What Is Next?

Although people in countries all over the world use coal every day, the world will not run out of coal anytime soon. Scientists say there is plenty of it still hidden below the Earth's surface—billions and billions of tons. In fact, researchers think the coal we have now

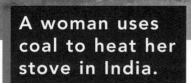

A woman uses coal to heat her stove in India.

will last for another two hundred years. By then, new coal seams will have formed. And geologists may have discovered easier ways to reach—and use—the coal we have already found.

Scientists are concerned with the way we use coal today, however. When coal and other fossil fuels are burned, they release dangerous gases—**carbon monoxide** and methane gas—into the

This power plant uses coal to create electricity.

air. These gases can cause explosions. They **pollute** the air with chemicals that are harmful to people, plants, and animals. These chemicals mix with the moisture in the clouds, becoming acid rain. Acid rain can poison our lakes and rivers. Today, coal is used much more safely than before. But scientists are still looking for ways to make it safer. They want to keep our air clean by reducing the

This scientist is working on a way to reduce the amount of gases released when coal is burned.

People will continue
to rely on coal for
many years to come.

gases that come from burning fossil fuels.

In the future, scientists hope to find new sources of energy and power that will not affect the environment. However, coal will always be one of our most important natural resources.

To Find Out More

Here are some additional resources to help you learn more about coal:

 **Books**

Bartoletti, Susan Campbell. **Growing Up In Coal Country.** Houghton-Mifflin Co., 1999.

Dineen, Jacqueline. **Oil, Gas, and Coal.** Raintree Steck-Vaughn Publishers, 1995.

Hansen, Michael C. **Coal: How It Is Found and Used.** Enslow Publishers, Inc., 1990.

Kittinger, Jo S. **A Look at Rocks: From Coal to Kimberlite.** Franklin Watts, 1998.

Spence, Margaret. **Fossil Fuels.** Gloucester Press / Aladdin Books, 1993.

Organizations and Online Sites

American Coal Foundation
1130 17th Street N.W.,
Suite 220
Washington, D.C.
20036-4604
http://www.acf-coal.org

This organization educates people about the coal industry.

Planetpals Earthzone
http://www.planetpals.com

This online site provides facts and fun activities about Earth.

United States Department of Energy
1000 Independence Avenue S.W.
Washington, D.C. 20585
http://www.energy.gov/ kidz/kidzone.html

This government agency offers a special section for kids to learn more about energy.

United States Environmental Protection Agency Explorers' Club for Kids
http://www.epa.gov/kids/

This online site supplies information about the environment as well as games and other fun activities.

Important Words

carbon a chemical ingredient found in every living thing and in coal and diamonds

carbon monoxide an odorless, colorless, dangerous gas

conveyor belt a belt that continuously carries objects from one place to another

decay to rot away and fall apart

detergent a soap-like substance used to clean things

fossil fuels fuels formed when the remains of plants and animals are crushed under layers of sedimentary rock

fuel a material which is burned to provide heat, light, or energy

geologist a scientist who studies rocks, minerals, and fossils to learn about the Earth

pollute to make something unclean or dirty